W9-CLN-069

STATE PROFILES

WYOMING

BY CHRISTINA LEAF

BLASTOFF!
DISCOVERY

BELLWETHER MEDIA • MINNEAPOLIS, MN

Blastoff! Discovery launches a new mission: reading to learn. Filled with facts and features, each book offers you an exciting new world to explore!

BLASTOFF! UNIVERSE

BLASTOFF! Beginners — GRADE K

BLASTOFF! READERS — GRADES 1-3

BLASTOFF! DISCOVERY — GRADE 4

This edition first published in 2022 by Bellwether Media, Inc.

No part of this publication may be reproduced in whole or in part without written permission of the publisher.
For information regarding permission, write to Bellwether Media, Inc., Attention: Permissions Department,
6012 Blue Circle Drive, Minnetonka, MN 55343.

Library of Congress Cataloging-in-Publication Data

Names: Leaf, Christina, author.
Title: Wyoming / by Christina Leaf.
Description: Minneapolis, MN : Bellwether Media, Inc., 2022. |
   Series: Blastoff! Discovery: State profiles | Includes bibliographical
   references and index. | Audience: Ages 7-13 | Audience: Grades
   4-6 | Summary: "Engaging images accompany information
   about Wyoming. The combination of high-interest subject matter
   and narrative text is intended for students in grades 3 through 8"–
   Provided by publisher.
Identifiers: LCCN 2021019703 (print) | LCCN 2021019704 (ebook)
   | ISBN 9781644873571 (library binding) |
   ISBN 9781648342004 (ebook)
Subjects: LCSH: Wyoming–Juvenile literature.
Classification: LCC F761.3 .L43 2022 (print) | LCC F761.3 (ebook) |
   DDC 978.7–dc23
LC record available at https://lccn.loc.gov/2021019703
LC ebook record available at https://lccn.loc.gov/2021019704

Editor: Kate Moening   Designer: Andrea Schneider

Printed in the United States of America, North Mankato, MN.

TABLE OF CONTENTS

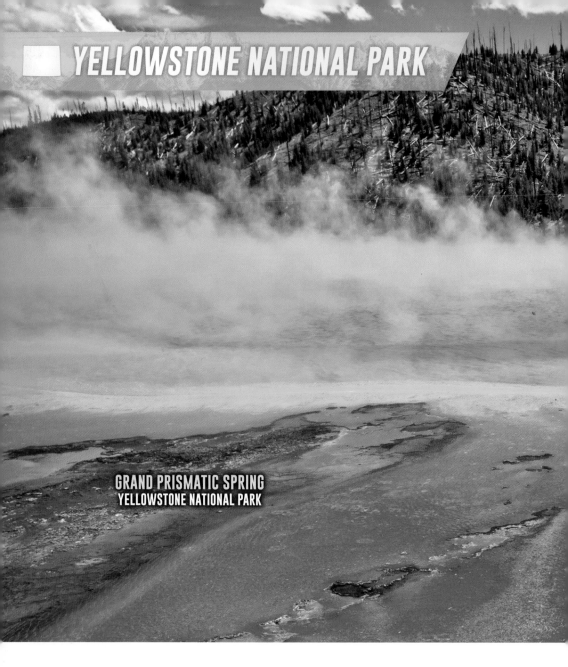

GRAND PRISMATIC SPRING
YELLOWSTONE NATIONAL PARK

A family drives into Yellowstone National Park. Around them, spouts of steam rise up across the landscape. They stop by Old Faithful and watch the famous **geyser** shoot water more than 130 feet (40 meters) into the air. Next, the family heads up the road to Grand Prismatic Spring. They take in the bright colors of the steaming **hot spring**.

A HOT SPOT

Yellowstone is on top of a supervolcano. Hot melted rock lies just underneath the surface there. This hotspot creates the park's geysers and hot springs.

DEVILS TOWER

FORT LARAMIE

GRAND TETON NATIONAL PARK

INDEPENDENCE ROCK

On their way out of the park, the family passes through the Lamar Valley. Herds of bison cross the road while a bald eagle soars overhead. In the distance, the family spots a grizzly bear disappearing into the forest. Welcome to Wyoming!

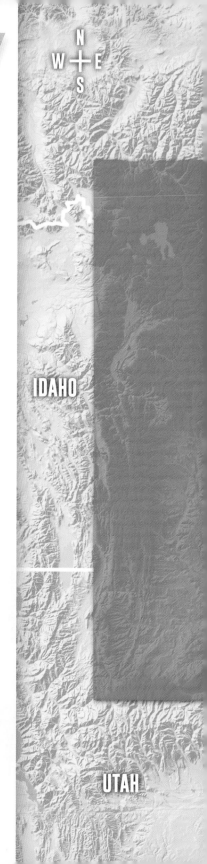

IDAHO

UTAH

Wyoming is a rectangular state in the western United States. It covers 97,813 square miles (253,335 square kilometers). The Rocky Mountains run through the western part of the state.

Montana borders Wyoming to the north. South Dakota and Nebraska make up its eastern border, and Colorado lies to the south. Utah hugs Wyoming's southwestern corner. Idaho is to the west of Wyoming. The capital city, Cheyenne, is in the southeastern corner near Colorado.

MONTANA

GILLETTE
●

SOUTH
DAKOTA ——

WYOMING

CASPER
●

NEBRASKA ——

LARAMIE
●   CHEYENNE
★

COLORADO

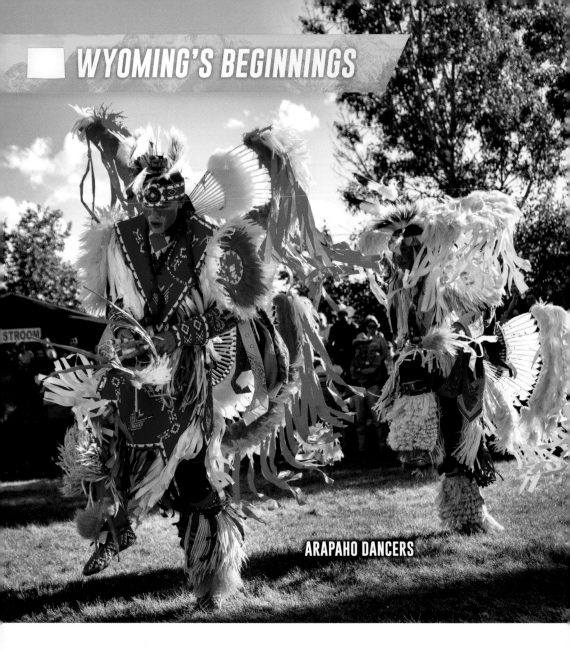

ARAPAHO DANCERS

People have lived in Wyoming for at least 12,000 years. Various people groups moved in and out of the area, following animals to hunt. These groups included the Shoshone, Arapaho, Crow, Cheyenne, and Ute peoples.

French explorers entered the area in the mid-1700s. Fur trappers arrived after the United States bought most of the land in the **Louisiana Purchase** in 1803. In the 1840s, **pioneers** moving westward through Wyoming began a lasting conflict between Native Americans and **settlers**. More people arrived with the construction of the Union Pacific Railroad in the 1860s. In 1890, Wyoming became the 44th state.

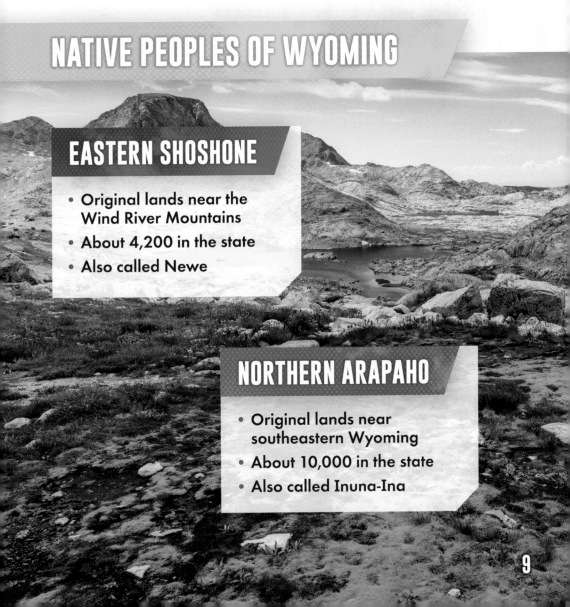

NATIVE PEOPLES OF WYOMING

EASTERN SHOSHONE

- Original lands near the Wind River Mountains
- About 4,200 in the state
- Also called Newe

NORTHERN ARAPAHO

- Original lands near southeastern Wyoming
- About 10,000 in the state
- Also called Inuna-Ina

Wyoming is divided between the Rocky Mountains and the **Great Plains**. The western part of the state is covered by the Rocky Mountains. The jagged Wind River Range and the striking Tetons lie within this region. Mountain streams from Wyoming's Rockies feed into many rivers, including the Missouri and the Colorado.

N
W + E
S

ROCKY MOUNTAINS   GREAT PLAINS
WIND RIVER RANGE

TETONS

DEVILS TOWER

SPRING
HIGH: 56°F (13°C)
LOW: 31°F (-1°C)

SUMMER
HIGH: 82°F (28°C)
LOW: 51°F (11°C)

FALL
HIGH: 58°F (14°C)
LOW: 32°F (0°C)

WINTER
HIGH: 36°F (2°C)
LOW: 14°F (-10°C)

°F = degrees Fahrenheit
°C = degrees Celsius

ROCK ON

Devils Tower is a huge rock formation in northeastern Wyoming. It is famous for its unique columns. These formed from melted rock that contracted as it cooled.

The wide grasslands of the Great Plains span the eastern part of the state. In the northeast, the Black Hills dip into Wyoming. Wyoming is generally dry and sunny. Winters are usually cold, and summers are warm. Rain and snow fall in the mountains, while the Great Plains are drier.

Wildlife is plentiful in Wyoming. Pronghorn leap across the Great Plains, while prairie falcons soar overhead. Black-footed ferrets and prairie dogs dig below the surface. Above ground, greater sage-grouses perform fancy dances. River otters play in Wyoming's rivers where cutthroat trout swim.

Yellowstone National Park is home to hundreds of species. This includes the largest bison population anywhere on public lands. Packs of wolves hunt elk and deer in the park. Bighorn sheep and mountain goats climb rocky slopes. Grizzly bears wander mountain forests, while black bears search for berries.

PRONGHORN

BLACK-TAILED PRAIRIE DOGS

GREATER SAGE-GROUSE

GRIZZLY BEAR

GRAY WOLVES

HOME ON THE RANGE

Bison have lived continuously in
Yellowstone for thousands of years!
It is the only place in the United States
that can make this claim.

AMERICAN BISON

Life Span: up to 20 years
Status: near threatened

American bison range =

LEAST CONCERN	NEAR THREATENED	VULNERABLE	ENDANGERED	CRITICALLY ENDANGERED	EXTINCT IN THE WILD	EXTINCT

Wyoming has the smallest population of all 50 states. Fewer than 600,000 people live there. Most Wyomingites have European backgrounds. Hispanic Americans make up the next-largest group. Small numbers of Asian Americans and Black or African Americans live in the state. The Shoshone and Arapaho are the largest Native American groups still in Wyoming. Many of them live on the Wind River **Reservation** in the west-central part of the state.

RESIDENTS OF THE WIND RIVER RESERVATION

WYOMING'S FUTURE: AN AGING POPULATION

Wyoming's population is aging quickly. This means there will be fewer people to fill the workforce. Health care will also become costly for the older citizens.

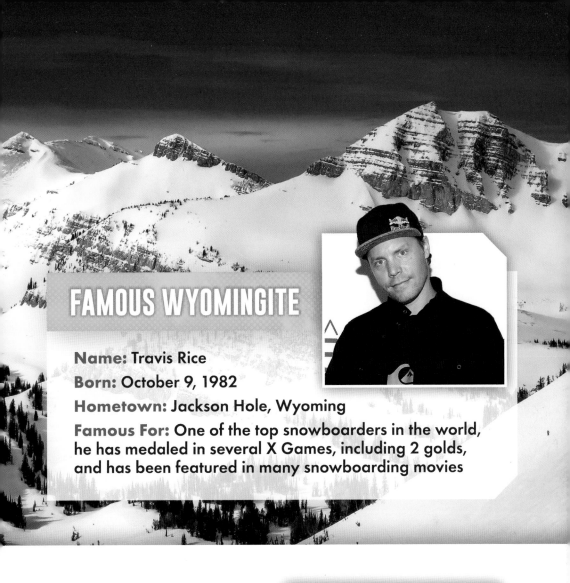

FAMOUS WYOMINGITE

Name: Travis Rice
Born: October 9, 1982
Hometown: Jackson Hole, Wyoming
Famous For: One of the top snowboarders in the world, he has medaled in several X Games, including 2 golds, and has been featured in many snowboarding movies

More than 6 out of every 10 Wyomingites live in and around cities. Cheyenne, Wyoming's largest city, has about 63,000 people. Other Wyomingites live in **rural** areas.

JACKSON

Named after Native Americans in the area, Cheyenne began as a stop on the Union Pacific Railroad in 1867. The city grew quickly. Rowdy townspeople and **saloons** made it a classic Wild West town. But the railroad also brought art and wealthy **investors**. Cheyenne became Wyoming's capital in 1869.

Today, Cheyenne is Wyoming's largest city. Just outside of the city lies F.E. Warren, a major Air Force base. Cheyenne celebrates its Western history with the Wyoming State Museum and Cheyenne Frontier Days. The world's largest **steam engine**, Big Boy Number 4004, reminds visitors of Cheyenne's railroad days.

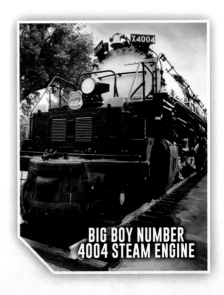

BIG BOY NUMBER 4004 STEAM ENGINE

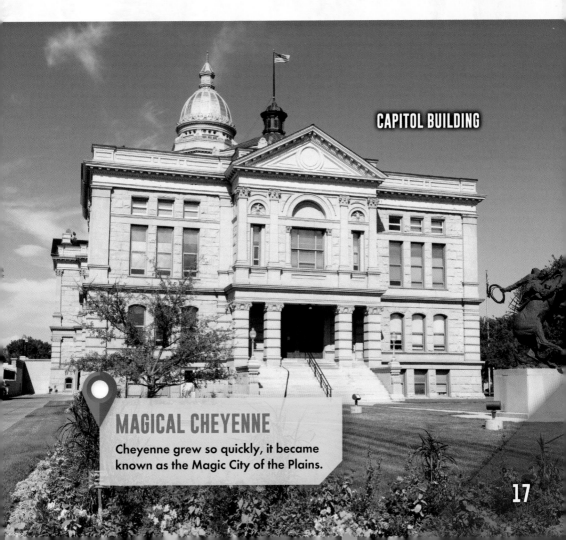

CAPITOL BUILDING

MAGICAL CHEYENNE

Cheyenne grew so quickly, it became known as the Magic City of the Plains.

17

Wyoming is famous for its cowboy history. Cattle ranches still cover much of the state. They bring in most of the farming income. Hay and sugar beets are top crops. Most people in Wyoming have **service jobs**. Many work in the national parks. They serve the millions of **tourists** that visit each year.

PARK RANGER

Much of Wyoming's economy depends on its **natural resources**. Coal was the most important resource early in Wyoming's history. Natural gas and petroleum are now more important. Miners in Wyoming pull these valuable resources from the earth. Workers in factories turn resources into new products, such as cement and wool.

WYOMING'S FUTURE: FOSSIL FUELS

Fossil fuels such as coal, natural gas, and petroleum are a major part of Wyoming's economy. However, the country is moving toward cleaner energy. Wyoming will need to find ways to adapt to the country's changing needs.

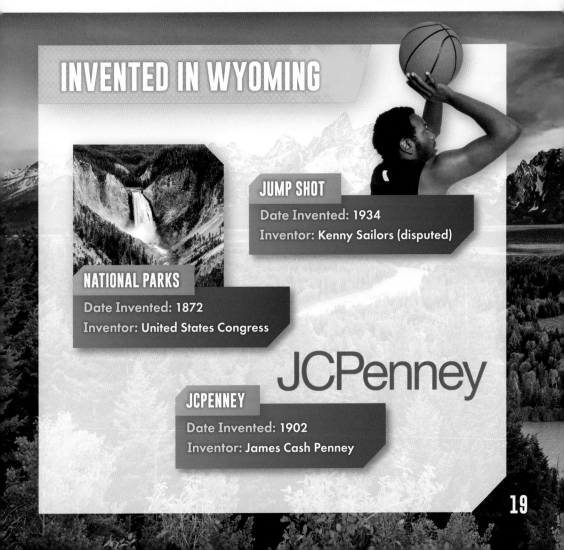

INVENTED IN WYOMING

JUMP SHOT
Date Invented: 1934
Inventor: Kenny Sailors (disputed)

NATIONAL PARKS
Date Invented: 1872
Inventor: United States Congress

JCPenney

JCPENNEY
Date Invented: 1902
Inventor: James Cash Penney

GRILLED BEEF

Wyoming's food borrows heavily from its cowboy past. People enjoy beef from Wyoming's many ranches. They may cook it over the grill, chicken fry it, or turn it into jerky. Many meals feature hearty cowboy dishes such as stews and chilis. The classic ranch favorite, biscuits and gravy, is a popular breakfast food.

CHUCKWAGON DINNERS

Some places in Wyoming offer chuckwagon dinners. These are based on old cowboy traditions. People gather around an old-fashioned wagon for food, music, and storytelling.

Enthusiasm for the outdoors also drives food in Wyoming. People enjoy wild game such as elk and bison. Trout caught from Wyoming's many rivers is also popular. Pies and jams often feature chokecherries from around the state.

BISON BURGER

CHOKECHERRIES

BISCUITS AND GRAVY

2 SERVINGS

Have an adult help you with this cowboy-inspired breakfast!

INGREDIENTS

1/4 pound pork sausage

2 tablespoons butter

2 to 3 tablespoons flour

1/4 teaspoon salt

1/8 teaspoon pepper

1 1/4 to 1 1/3 cup warm milk

warm biscuits

DIRECTIONS

1. Cook the sausage over medium heat and then drain.

2. Add the butter and let it melt.

3. Add the flour, salt, and pepper. Cook and stir until well mixed.

4. Stir in the milk, and bring to a boil. Stir for about 2 minutes until thickened.

5. Serve immediately over biscuits.

RODEO

Wyoming is famous for its rodeos! Crowds gather to watch cowboys and cowgirls show off their riding and roping skills. Cowboys and Cowgirls are also the mascots of the University of Wyoming's sports teams. People cheer on their basketball and football teams. High school teams draw fans as well.

COWBOYS MASCOT

Wyoming offers plenty to do outdoors. In summer, millions of people hike and camp in Yellowstone and Grand Teton National Parks. Wyomingites fish for trout or whitewater raft on the state's many rivers. Fall draws hunters to the woods to look for deer. In winter, people hit the mountains to ski and snowboard.

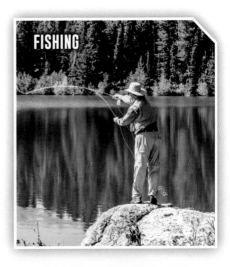

FISHING

NOTABLE SPORTS TEAM

University of Wyoming Cowboys
Sport: National Collegiate Athletic Association basketball
Started: 1904
Place of Play: Arena-Auditorium

SHOSHONE POWWOW

Festivals fill the year in Wyoming! Native American groups such as the Shoshone host **powwows** in spring and summer. People dress in **traditional** clothing and perform **ceremonial** dances. Wyomingites celebrate the ways of trappers during the 1838 Mountain Man **Rendezvous** in summer. People try skills like tomahawk throwing, starting fires with flint, and setting traps.

Late July brings the world's largest outdoor rodeo to Wyoming during Cheyenne Frontier Days. People enjoy watching bull riding, concerts, and gunfight reenactments. Families take in Wyoming's history in the Indian Village and Old Frontier Town. Wyoming has many ways to celebrate its past!

JACKSON HOLE FALL ARTS FESTIVAL

September brings art lovers to the Jackson Hole Fall Arts Festival. Visitors wander through fairs and galleries to look at paintings, jewelry, and other art.

CHEYENNE FRONTIER DAYS

25

1869

The Wyoming territory grants women the right to vote, more than 50 years before the rest of the country

PRE-1700s

Many nomadic Native American groups, including the Shoshone and the Arapaho, live in the area that is now Wyoming

1854

The Grattan Massacre becomes one of the first major events in the Plains Indian Wars

1868

The U.S. government and Arapaho people sign a treaty that promises the Arapaho a reservation, but the reservation is never actually created

1743

French explorers first arrive in Wyoming

1872

Yellowstone becomes the first national park in the U.S. and the world

1878

The Arapaho people are sent to live on the Wind River Reservation with the Shoshone people

1925

Nellie Tayloe Ross becomes the first female governor in the United States

2005

Wyoming creates a fund to protect wildlife and the environment

1890

Wyoming becomes the 44th state

1970s

Wyoming's population grows rapidly due to a mining boom

Nicknames: The Equality State, Big Wyoming, The Cowboy State

Motto: Equal Rights

Date of Statehood: July 10, 1890 (the 44th state)

Capital City: Cheyenne ★

Other Major Cities: Casper, Laramie, Gillette

Area: 97,813 square miles (253,335 square kilometers); Wyoming is the 10th largest state.

Population

576,851

(2020)

STATE FLAG

Wyoming's flag is blue with a red border. The blue stands for justice and Wyoming's landscape, and red represents the blood of pioneers and Native Americans. In the center of the flag, the state seal sits on a white bison. The white stands for purity. The state seal includes the motto and a woman for the state's history of political rights. It also has a cowboy and a miner for the state's major industries.

INDUSTRY

Main Exports

beef

chemicals

machinery

metal products

hay

sugar beets

JOBS

MANUFACTURING
3%

FARMING AND NATURAL RESOURCES
11%

GOVERNMENT
19%

SERVICES
67%

Natural Resources
coal, natural gas, petroleum, uranium

GOVERNMENT

Federal Government

1 REPRESENTATIVE | **2** SENATORS

WY

3 ELECTORAL VOTES

USA

State Government

60 REPRESENTATIVES | **30** SENATORS

STATE SYMBOLS

STATE BIRD
WESTERN MEADOWLARK

STATE MAMMAL
AMERICAN BISON

STATE FLOWER
WYOMING INDIAN PAINTBRUSH

STATE TREE
PLAINS COTTONWOOD

GLOSSARY

ceremonial—related to a ceremony; a ceremony is a formal act or event that is part of a social or religious occasion.

geyser—a spring that shoots out jets of hot water or steam

Great Plains—a region of flat or gently rolling land in the central United States

hot spring—a place where hot water flows out of the ground

investors—people who put money into a project in hopes of earning more money later

Louisiana Purchase—a deal made between France and the United States; it gave the United States 828,000 square miles (2,144,510 square kilometers) of land west of the Mississippi River.

natural resources—materials in the earth that are taken out and used to make products or fuel

pioneers—people who are among the first to explore or settle in an area

powwows—Native American gatherings that usually include dancing

rendezvous—a planned meeting

reservation—an area of land that is controlled by Native American tribes

rural—related to the countryside

saloons—bars or pubs

service jobs—jobs that perform tasks for people or businesses

settlers—people who come to live in a new, undeveloped region

steam engine—an engine that generates power with steam

tourists—people who travel to visit another place

traditional—related to customs, ideas, or beliefs handed down from one generation to the next

AT THE LIBRARY

Lauryssens, Molly. *Intro to Rodeo*. Minneapolis, Minn.: Abdo Pub., 2018.

Orr, Tamra B. *Yellowstone*. New York, N.Y.: AV2 by Weigl, 2020.

Wallace, Audra. *Wyoming*. New York, N.Y.: Children's Press, 2019.

ON THE WEB

FACTSURFER

Factsurfer.com gives you a safe, fun way to find more information.

1. Go to www.factsurfer.com.

2. Enter "Wyoming" into the search box and click 🔍.

3. Select your book cover to see a list of related content.

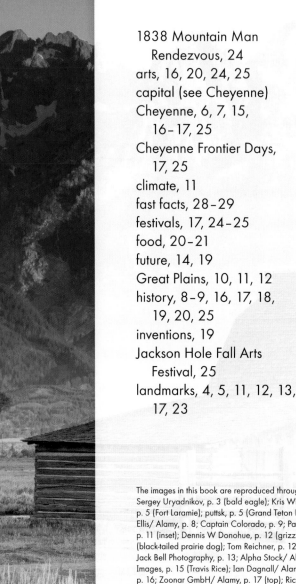